Windows 8

100 Tips to Become a PRO in No Time

Disclaimer

What Will You Find In This Book?

Launched just a few months back, Windows 8 caused a commotion in the IT industry. It is said to be the most dynamic operating system launched by Microsoft. Windows 8 is different and far more exciting than its predecessors. It has innumerous features and utilities that are not only unique but also very user friendly.

The fact that you are reading this book implies that you probably have already experienced Windows 8 and are looking for ways to explore more of it.

Well you have definitely come to the right place. This book is not a typical user guide teaching you the basics of Windows 8. It contains **100 exciting unique tips** that will make you love Windows 8 even more.

Want to peek on the few tips? Well, here it is.

Some of the most exciting tips of this book include the following.

1. Let your creativity flow while setting up your password

2. The secret to install the traditional evergreen all-time popular start button

3. Easy-to-remember keyboard shortcuts and mouse gestures

4. Some amazing tips on protection and personalization

5. Ways to save the data usage and bandwidth

And much more…

So don't just stop here. Continue reading and explore Windows 8 all over again.

Contents

Tip # 1: Be Creative with Your Password

Let your creativity flow while creating your password

Windows 8 has many exciting features including the picture password feature. You will be given a default password the first time you install windows 8 on your PC. However you can change that password later on.

1. Go to **Settings**

2. Tap/Click **PC settings**

3. Tap/Click your user account

4. Tap/Click **Create a Picture Password**

5. Enter the default password

6. Once you do that, a window will open up on the screen. Select the picture that you want to set up in the password.

7. Now select three different points on the image and make any symbol or shape on the selected points. You can make circles, straight lines or simple tap at the particular points.

8. Tap/Click **Finish**

Every time you log in to your account, you will have to make the same symbol on the same points to unlock the screen.

Tip # 2: Clear Up the Screen Animations

Animations looks wonderful, however they become annoying at times especially when you are using a portable device and a particular animation consumes too much of the battery. You can turn off the animations whenever you want.

1. Go to Control Panel

2. Tap/Click **System and Security**

3. Tap/Click **Advanced System Settings > Settings**

4. Go to the **Performance tab** and unmark **Animate windows when minimizing and maximizing**

Tip # 3: How to Modify Your Account Details

1. Login as administrator. This step is necessary to make changes in any of the user accounts.

2. Go to **Control Panel**

3. Click/tap **User Accounts**.

4. Tap/click the particular user account you wish to modify the detail of

5. A new window will open up allowing you to change account information including the account title, password, picture, family safety settings etcetera.

Tip # 4: Print with Windows 8

Printing is a very commonly needed feature needed by almost every computer user. And Windows 8 has made it very easy and effective. It features an advanced driver architecture called version 4, shortly read as v4. This tool has simplified the printer installation process. Now you don't need to locate any driver on your PC/tablet. Just connect your printer to your system. Windows 8 will find the best driver available for the particular printer and the installation will start automatically. Once the installation is done, just open the document you wish to get the hard copy and enter the command to print.

Tip # 5: Quick Transfer of Files with Windows 8

Another very accommodating feature of the Windows 8 is the **Windows Easy Transfer** feature. As the name suggests, this feature enables quick and easy transfer of files from your old PC/tablet to the new one containing Windows 8. Not only files, you can also transfer the setting to your new system. Just make sure that both your PCs are free of any viruses and malware before executing the transfer.

To transfer files via the Windows Easy Transfer,

1. Install Windows Easy Transfer on your old and new PC

2. To connect both the systems via the Easy Transfer wire or any other external cable or hard drive.

3. Open the **Windows Easy Transfer** in PC containing Windows 8

4. Click **Next**

5. Select your **transfer method**

6. Click **This is my new PC**

7. Now open Windows Easy Transfer in your old PC

8. Click **Next**

9. Select the same transfer method

All the selected files will be transferred automatically

Tip # 6: Reveal/Hide Your Password

Windows 8 contains a password reveal feature that allows you to reveal or hide the password as you type. To enable/disable this feature,

1. Make sure you are log in as administrator

2. Tap/hit **Windows key + R** on your keyboard

3. Type **gpedit.msc.**

4. Once you do that, you will be taken to the Local Group Policy Editor page

5. Go to **Computer Configuration**

6. Select **Administrative Template**

7. Click/Tap **Windows Component > Credential User Interface**

8. Click/Tap **Do not display the password reveal button**

9. Click **Enabled** to hide the password while you type. You can disable this option in the same way.

Tip # 7: Shortcut to Shutdown

You might be thinking what is so un que about shutdown that we included it here as part of the 100 tips. Well, as you must have noticed by now that Windows 8 does not have the typical Start button that contains the option to shutdown. A new user may have a tough time finding the shutdown button in Windows 8.

So here is the shortcut: **Alt+F4.** Once you hit this combination, a small window asking *"What do you want the computer to do?"* will pop up on the screen. Tap/Click **shutdown**.

There is another way to shut down your Windows 8 system.

1. Open the charms bar

2. Tap/click **Settings**

3. Tap/click the power button.

4. Select **shutdown** from the list of available options.

Tip # 8: Refresh Without Formatting

If any virus or malware has penetrated your Windows 8 is not working smoothly due to any other reason, you can always refresh it without having to format all the data and settings. To do so,

1. Open the **Charms b**ar

2. Go to **Settings**

3. Click/Tap **Change** PC settings

4. Click/Tap **General**

5. Click/Tap **Refresh your PC without affecting your files** > **Get started**

6. Follow the onscreen instructions to refresh your PC.

The most amazing part about this procedure is that all the apps that were preinstalled in your PC or that you downloaded from the Windows Store will be reinstalled automatically after the system refresh is complete. You will only have to reinstall the third party apps.

Tip # 9: How to Access Your Personal Email in Windows 8

Windows 8 features a very advanced and interactive email app. It allows you to access all your email accounts from one place. Here is how you can do it.

1. Go to the Start Screen

2. Open the email app

3. Go the **settings** > **Accounts**

4. Click/Tap **Add an account**

5. A list of all the major email service providers will be displayed on the screen. Click/Tap the service provider of whom you want to access the emails.

6. Enter your email ID, password and any other required details.

You can add as many email accounts as you want in the same manner.

Tip # 10: The Quick Search Tip

Are you looking for a particular file that is lost in hundreds and thousands of files/folders? Here is a quick and simple way of finding it.

Open the file explorer. Then enter the name of the file you are looking for, in the search box. You don't have to enter the complete and exact title. Any keyword will do. You can filter your search by entering the file type (such as .docx or .xls)

Windows will generate the list of all the files that matches your search criteria.

Tip # 11: Know Your Location with Windows 8

Windows 8 features a built-in Maps app powered by Bing. It allows you to view you favorite locations around the globe. However it does not show the street view. But you can do so by installing Google Maps from the Windows App store.

This way you can view all the location around the world with their street view. This is not it! By turning on the GPS, you can also find your own location. This app is very helpful when you are in a new place or are lost somewhere.

Tip # 12: Restore For Proper Functioning

If your PC or tablet containing Windows 8 is not functioning properly, you can restore it back to the previous condition where it was working smoothly. Likewise, if you installed an App that slowed down your PC or laptop, you can use the System Restore feature to nullify the App's effects.

To access the Windows 8 System Restore,

1. Hit the **Windows key + W**

2. Search for restore point

3. Click/Tap **Create a Restore point** from the search results

4. You will be asked to select a drive on your system

5. Click/Tap the **Configure button**. This will start the system restore on your selected drive. You can also set the space limit for the restore points.

To restore your system to any previous point,

1. Hit the **Alt key + S**

2. Click/Tap the **restore point** you want to use

It will take a couple of minutes or more for the restore process to execute completely. Make sure you do it when you are not in a hurry.

Tip # 13: Sleep And Save

You can save the battery of your laptop from draining by putting is to sleep whenever it's not in use. The easiest way to do is by closing its lid. However you cannot do so if you are using PC.

To put your PC to sleep, you just have to press the power button. However in order to do this way, you need to modify the settings a bit.

1. Access the charms bar

2. Click or Tap the **PC settings**

3. Select the **Power Options**

4. Select **Choose what the power button does if you're using a desktop or tablet.**

5. Click/Tap **Sleep**

If you are using a laptop, then the first 3 steps remain the same. After that, you need to select **Choose what closing the lid does**

Click/Tap **Sleep** in front of both the options; when your laptop is running on battery and when the laptop is plugged in.

Tip # 14: Easy Synchronization of Files with Windows 8

Now this is one of the most amazing features of Windows 8. You don't have to transfer all your files and settings every time you use a different device.

Windows 8 allows you to sync all your files, folders, preferences, settings and themes with all the devices that have Windows 8. All this is possible through the Microsoft Account Integration tool.

You just need to sign up for your Microsoft user ID. Once you get that, the rest is pretty simple.

Whenever you are using Windows 8 on any other device, all you have to do is sign-in using your Microsoft account ID and password. All your personalized settings and selected files will automatically be synced with the particular device.

Tip # 15: Share with Other Users

Another very exciting feature of Windows 8 is that it allows you to share your files and folders among other user accounts. The process to do this is very simple and easy.

1. First you need to log in as Administrator, if you are logged in from any other user account.

2. Open the *file explorer*

3. Select the file or folder that you want to share

4. Go the *File Explorer Ribbon* and Tap/Click the **Share** tab

5. Choose the forum where you want to share the selected files

6. It is up to you if want to share it with one or all the users of your *Homegroup*

7. If you are sharing any important or critical drive/folder, make sure to use the *Advanced Security option*

Tip # 16: Sort out Your Desktop

If you desktop is very messy, loaded with shortcuts and folders and you are just too lazy to sort it up, let Windows 8 does it for you. You just have to permit it.

Here is how you can do it.

1. Right click your desktop

2. Select **Sort By**

3. You will see a number of options for sorting up your desktop. You can arrange the icons by size, name, date and type. Select either one.

4. You can also select the Auto Arrange Icons. If you go for this option, all the icons on your desktop will be lined up in neat vertical rows.

Tip # 17: One Click Private Browsing

Another very exciting and popular feature of Windows 8 is that it allows you to do private browsing in IE 10. And it is just a one click process. To start a private browsing session in IE 10, all you have to do is hit the **Windows key + Z**.

Tip # 18: How to Install Third Party Apps

If you don't find your required app in the Windows App Store or you want to download any third party app, Windows 8 allows you to do that. It does not restrict you to its own App store only.

To install third party or non-store apps in Windows 8,

1. Go to the start screen and search for **Run**

2. Once the Run Command Prompt is opened, type gpedit.msc and hit **Enter**

3. You will be taken to the *Local Group Policy Editor*

4. Go to **Computer Configuration** > **Administrative Templates**

5. Tap/Click the **Windows Component** than hit **App Package Deployment**

6. Select **Allow all trusted apps to install** > **Enabled**

7. Click or Tap **Apply** then hit **OK**

Now you are ready to install third party apps in your Windows 8.

You can download any number of third party apps you want. Just make sure it is from a reliable source. Downloading apps from unknown sources can cause damage to your PC/tablet in terms of virus, malwares or illegal security breach.

Make sure have an updated antivirus app and scan the app immediately after downloading it. Also, it is recommended that you keep the Windows Defender turned on at all time to keep your system protected from potential cyber threats.

Tip # 19: Switch to the Desktop View

The most popular thing about Windows 8 is its unique interface and Live Tiles Desktop View. However many people don't find it that attractive and are comfortable with the traditional Windows desktop.

Well, you don't have to compromise on all the exciting features of Windows 8 just because you don't like its default desktop view. You can switch to the old desktop view just by hitting **Start + D**. Hit the same keys again to switch back to the Windows 8 Live Tiles desktop.

Tip # 20: Let Your Windows 8 Maintain Itself

Windows 8 contains an amazing Automatic Maintenance tool. It features the remarkable Software Update, Automatic Security Scan and System Diagnostics tool. All these tools combined takes care of your Windows 8 even when you are not using your PC/laptop.

To activate the automatic maintenance system,

1. Go the *control panel* or access the *taskbar*

2. Click/Tap the **Action Center ico**n

3. Click/Tap **Maintenance** > **Start Maintenance**

You can also set the time of the day when you want the Automatic Maintenance to take place.

To set your desired time for automatic maintenance, click or tap **Change Maintenance Settings** and then choose your desired time.

To disable the automatic maintenance feature,

1. Go the *control panel* or access the *taskbar*

2. Click/Tap the **Action Center ico**n

3. Click/Tap **Maintenance** > **Stop Maintenance**

4. Close the action center

Tip # 21: Install the Traditional Start Button

Just like the old desktop view, Windows 8 users also miss the Traditional Start Button. However, you don't have to miss it anymore. There are a number of third party apps that installs the Start Button in Windows 8.

The third party apps that integrate the Start Button with Windows 8 include Start8, Vistart Menu, Classic Shell and IObit Start Men.

All the above mentioned apps are compatible with Windows 8. Some of them are free to use and some are premium. You will have to pay certain charges to use the premium apps.

Tip # 22: Activate/Deactivate the Lock Screen

Windows 8 allows you to enable or disable the Lock Screen. The process to do is very easy.

1. Tap/hit **Windows key + R** on your keyboard

2. Type **gpedit.msc.**

3. Once you do that, you will be taken to the *Local Group Policy Editor* page

4. If you wish to see the Lock Screen, Tap/Click **Disable > OK**. If you don't want to see the Lock Screen, Tap/Click **Enable > OK**.

The last step may sound confusing to you, but this is how it works. The *Group Policy Editor* works in the opposite manner. Therefore you need to hit **Enable** in order to deactivate the lock screen and vice versa.

Tip # 23: Customize Your Windows 8

When it comes to personalizing the lock screen, start screen and other such displays, Windows 8 has simply outdone all the others. The personalization feature in Windows 8 is very attractive and pretty easy to use.

1. First, go to PC Settings

2. Click/Tap **Personalize**

3. You will be taken to the Lock Screen settings. Choose the image that you want to see at the Lock Screen.

4. Next, Click/Tap the Start Screen tab. Here you can customize your Windows background.

5. Play with different colors and themes till you are satisfied with the final results.

6. Finally, Click/Tap the Account Picture tab.

7. Select the desired image that you want to up to for your User Account Display picture.

You can change these settings as many times as you want.

Tip # 24: Play With Shortcuts

Windows 8 is very exciting to use. It gets even more interesting once you are used to of certain shortcuts.

Shortcuts not only saves ones time but makes also exhilarates the experience of using Windows 8. Here are some really useful commonly used shortcuts.

Alt+F4: Close an app

Ctrl + Shift + Esc: Launch Task Manager

F5: Refresh the current screen

Shift key 5 times: To turn on/off the sticky notes

Windows Key + -: Zoom out

Windows Key + +: Zoom in

Windows key + B: Go back to desktop

Windows key + C: Open the charms bar

Windows key + D: Open Desktop

Windows Key + Down Arrow: Minimize the current window

Windows Key + E: Opens the Windows Explorer

Windows Key + Esc: Close the Magnifier

Windows key + F: Search files

Windows Key + F1: Launch Windows Help and Support

Windows key + H: Charms bar – Share

Windows key + I: Charms bar – Settings

Windows key + K: Charms bar – Devices

Windows Key + L: Lock PC/laptop and go to Lock Screen

Windows Key + M: Minimize all open windows

Windows key + R: Opens the dialog box for Run command

Windows Key + Shift + M: Restore all the minimized Windows

Windows Key + Up Arrow: Maximize the current window

Windows Key + V: Open notifications

Windows key + W: Search settings

Windows key + Z: Get to app options

Windows key +: Peek at desktop

Windows key +Q: Charms bar – Search

Tip # 25: Explore the Windows Store

The Windows 8 app store is full of entertaining and utility apps that you can download on your laptop, computer or tablet. The only requirement to explore this amazing app store is to have to a Microsoft live account, which most of us already have.

You can enter the Windows 8 app store by signing in your live account. Once you access the store, you will see that all the apps are divided into certain categories. Browse for your desired apps.

Once you locate the app you want to download, Tap/Click the Install icon. Once the download is completed, the particular app will appear in the notification panel as well as in the menu. Click/Tap to open and use the downloaded app.

Tip # 26: Stay Updated With Live Tiles

As already mentioned several times, Live Tile is the most unique and popular feature of Windows 8. It is the primary factor that makes Windows 8 stand apart from its predecessors.

Live Tile shows the updated status of the respective app. For example, if you have a stock market app installed on your PC/tablet, the live tile for this app will display the current position of the stock market.

To turn on/off the Live Tiles for a particular app,

1. Go to the Start Screen

2. Right Click the desired app

3. A small window will pop up at the bottom of your screen. Select Live Tile On or Off, whatever is it that you wish to do.

Live Tiles are very helpful for emails and other social media app. You don't have to check your email or Facebook after every few hours. The Live Tile for the particular app will keep you updated if any new message or notification arrives and if you really need to access the full app.

Tip # 27: Stay Connected

The People App in Windows 8 is unlike any other typical contact management app. It allows you to stay connected with your Facebook account without having to login every time you want to use Facebook.

To add and then sync your Facebook account with Windows 8,

1. Go the Start Screen

2. Click or tap the *People App*

3. Click/Tap **Settings**

4. Go the **Accounts** > **Facebook**

5. Enter your Facebook login details

6. Click/Tap **Done**

Likewise you can also add LinkedIn and Twitter accounts.

Tip # 28: Manage Multiple Machines with Hyper-V

Windows 8 features the remarkable virtualization technology Hyper-V that allows you to manage multiple computers/laptops from one machine. You just need to install Hyper-V and then you will be able to handle a number of machines from one just one main server.

Here is how you can do this.

1. Go to *Control Panel*

2. Click/Tap **Programs and Features**

3. Select Windows Features on/off

4. A small screen will open up. Here you will see that Hyper-V is deactivated by default.

5. Click/Tap the tiny plus icon next to Hyper-V.

6. Mark the checkboxes that appears below Hyper-V

7. Click/Tap **OK**

Hyper-V is successfully installed and ready to use.

Tip # 29: Explore Windows 8 in Your Language

Just like every other operating system, Windows 8 allows you to set your default language while installing in for the first time. But what is more interesting is that you can install a language pack anytime you want after the installation process

To change your default language,

1. Go to the Control Panel

2. Click/Tap **Languages**

3. Click/Tap **Add a Language Option**

4. A window will open up containing the list of different languages

5. Select your desired language

Your new language pack is successful installed.

Tip # 30: Pin To Protect

Surely your computer contains a lot of your personal stuff that you do not want others to see. Well, Windows 8 offers a very simple way of protecting your system.

You can use a pin code to protect your system. It works just like we set a pin protection code in smartphones. As a matter of fact, this one is ever more secured and interesting than the protection option in cell phones.

Windows 8 offers three ways of protection passwords. These include picture password, account password and pin password. We have already talked about the picture password in one of our previous tips.

To set the pin password,

1. Go to *PC settings*

2. Click/Tap **Users**

3. Click/Tap **Create a Pin**

4. Enter your old pin code

5. Now enter the new pin code (4-digit code that you can easily remember but cannot be easily guessed by others)

6. Reenter your new pin code to confirm

7. Click/Tap **Finish**

Tip # 31: Tip to Take Screenshot

If you come across any interesting webpage that you want to save for offline reading, the simplest way is to take its screenshot.

The typical way of taking the screer shot is the hit *print screen* > paste in *paint* and then save. Well, Windows 8 has made it pretty easy. It eliminates the paste and save step. All the screenshots are directly saved into the picture folder.

To take a screenshot in Windows 8,

1. Open the screen of which you want to take the screenshot

2. Press and hold for a few seconds, the **windows key plus PrtScn key** *(print screen).*

3. The screen may get dim for a few seconds. Don't worry it will come to normal as soon as the screenshot is clicked.

4. Your screenshot is saved in PNG format. Go to the Picture folder to view it.

Tip # 32: How to Clear Up Your Previous Entries

IE 10 maintains a record of your past history of browsing. This can be very helpful at times, especially when you need to browse the same pages frequently. However it can become potentially risky and harmful to your personal data if your computer or laptop is shared by multiple users.

To protect the privacy of your browsing history and preferences, it is very important that you clear the record of your previous entries regularly especially before allowing someone else to use your computer.

Here is how you can do it.

1. Open the IE 10 browser

2. Go to Internet Properties

3. Click/Tap the *content tab*

4. Click/Tap **Settings** next to the *Autocomplete tab*

5. Checkmark all the boxes

6. Click/Tap **Delete Autocomplete History**

Your browsing history cannot be seen by other users now.

Tip # 33: Find the Hibernate Option

If you are new to Windows 8, you may have a hard time finding the hibernate option as it is not in the list of restart and shutdown. It is not there by default but you can put it there by modifying the settings a bit.

Follow the below instructions to make the hibernate icon visible in the shutdown option list.

1. Go to *Control Panel*

2. Click/Tap **Power Options**

3. Click/Tap **Choose what the power buttons do**. You will find this option at the left side of the screen.

4. Click/Tap **Change settings.** These are the settings that are currently integrated in your computer.

5. Tick the box next to *Hibernate*

6. Click/Tap **Save Changes**

7. The hibernate option will now appear in the shutdown and restart option list.

Tip # 34: Upgrade to Windows 8

There are several ways of enjoying the latest operating system by Microsoft. You can experience the amazing Windows 8 by upgrading the old versions of Windows such as Windows 7, Windows XP or Windows Vista to Windows 8. Just make sure your device is compatible with the version you plan to install.

If you don't want to upgrade your old operating, you can also install it from Windows 8 installation DVD.

Whatever way you opt for, make sure you check out the official website of Microsoft amazing deals and upgrades. If you want to buy the latest operating system or any upgrade directly from Microsoft's site, you can so by visiting the **Download and Shop** page. There you will see an option **Buy Windows 8**. Click/tap the said option and it will install the Windows Upgrade Assistant on your laptop or PC.

Save and then run the upgrade assistant. First it will check if your system is compatible with the particular upgrade. Once the compatibility check is complete, the upgrade assistant will help you through the rest of the installation process.

Tip # 35: Remove Your PC from Windows Store

When you sign in to the Windows app store and install any app from it, your laptop/computer is automatically added to the Windows Store Account. You can add a maximum of five devices in one Windows Store Account.

If you want to install any app to a new PC or laptop which is not already added in the Windows Store Account, then you will have to first delete any your old PC/laptop from there. Here is how you can do it.

1. Go to the *Start Screen*

2. Click/tap the *windows Store icon*

3. If you are not already signed in the windows app store, do it using your Microsoft account details

4. Now open the charms bar

5. Click/Tap **Settings** > **Your Account**

6. You will see the list of all the PCs and laptops that are added in the Windows Store Account. Locate the device that you want to remove and Click/Tap **Remove** under it.

7. Click/Tap **Confirm**

Now you can add another PC to your Windows Store Account. Just remember one thing: You won't be able to use the apps you installed on the device that you just removed from the account.

Tip # 36: Windows 8 And The New Metro UI

The biggest change and attraction in Windows 8 is its new Metro User Interface (UI). This is the primary factor that makes Windows 8 stand apart from its predecessors. Before the launch of Windows 8, we were all used to the idea of 'desktop', the main page that is the starting route to everything that the OS and computer has.

Well, the revolutionary Windows 8 changed the concept of this typical desktop. It features a Start Screen with Live Tiles. It is this start screen that is base of desktop in Windows 8.

As mentioned in one of the previous tips, you can toggle between the old desktop view and Live Tiles start screen. However mostly users are attracted by the latter.

Tip # 37: Settings for Metro Apps

First you need to know what Metro Apps are. Though all of us know what it is, we just don't recognize it by this name. Metro Apps are nothing but the apps that you install from the Windows App Store.

The fact that this name is so uncommon is because Microsoft has officially renamed *Metro Apps* as *Windows Store Apps*. Also it allows you to change the privacy settings of individual Metro Apps for your own account.

Following is the step by step tutorial on how you can do it.

1. First, you need to select the app for which you want to change the privacy settings.

2. Next, reveal the charms bar.

3. Tap/click **Settings**

4. A small menu will appear at the top right corner of the screen. Tap/click **Permissions**.

5. Turn the permissions on/off, whatever is it that you wish to do.

6. Once you are done with this, come back to the Start Screen.

7. Repeat the same for as many Metro Apps as you want.

Tip # 38: Uninstall Unwanted Apps

As you must have experienced by now, Windows 8 contains uncountable free and paid apps. While you have to be a bit sure and thorough when buying paid apps, the same does not apply in case of free apps.

Download as many apps as you want. Even if you are not sure if the particular app is good, just install it anyways. You can delete it easily.

There are two ways of deleting the unwanted apps. The first one is explained as follows.

1. Go the start screen

2. Right click on the app you want to uninstall

3. Tap/click **Uninstall** from the right click menu

4. The particular app will be deleted within a few seconds.

If you are unable to find the particular app, go for this second way.

1. Go the start screen

2. Right click anywhere on the screen

3. Click/tap **All Apps** from the small window that appears at the bottom of the screen.

4. Search for the app you want to uninstall.

5. Right click on the particular app and hit **Uninstall** from the right click menu.

The particular app will be permanently removed from your system. You can reinstall it if you want from the Windows app store.

Tip # 39: Protect User Accounts

If your computer or laptop is shared by multiple users, then it would be better if you set up a password for every user account. Though it is not necessary, it is highly recommended for security purpose.

Here is what you need to do to set up a password for every user account.

1. Log in as administrator

2. Go to Control Panel

3. Click/tap **User Accounts** > **Manage Another Account**

4. Select the user account for which you want to set up the password.

5. Click/tap **Create A Password**. You will find this option at the side bar

6. Enter the password (that can be easily remembered by you but not so easily guessed by others)

7. Re-enter the same password to confirm

8. Enter a password hint (This step is optional. It is just to remind you of your password in case you forget it)

9. Click/tap **Create Password**

The particular user account is protected now.

Tip # 40: Modify Your Data Usage Plan for Live Apps

The Windows App Store features the automatic update feature for live apps. It updates all the live apps automatically whenever any new update is available.

Though this feature saves time, it may become quite burdensome and expensive if the updates consume lots of your monthly internet usage. However it does not mean that you can or should not avail this amazing feature. You can limit your data usage for every month and this way the automatic updates won't exceed the set limit.

To customize your data usage plan, you need to modify the settings for live updates.

1. Go to the Start screen

2. Open the charms bar

3. Tap/click **Settings**

4. Select the live tiles from the menu that appears on the screen

5. Determine the amount of data you want to allocate for live updates

That's it! You don't have to worry about excess data usage now.

Tip # 41: Browsing In Safe Mode

If your system is facing any minor bugs or errors, try running it in *Safe Mode*. Here is how you can do that.

1. Go to the Start screen

2. Open the charms bar

3. Type **Advanced Startup** in the search bar

4. Go to the *advanced setup*

5. Tap/click **Restart** Now

6. Tap/click **Troubleshoot Option**

7. Tap/click **Windows Startup Settings** > **Restart**

8. Wait for a few seconds, till a new menu appears containing the *Advanced Boot Options*

9. Hit **Safe Mode** and this should be it!

Tip # 42: Auto Update IE 10

Windows 8 features the amazing IE 10 that contains everything that you would want in a web browser. The IE 10 auto update tool is set to on by default.

To turn it off,

1. Open the IE 10 web browser

2. In the top right corner of screen, you will see a small pointed wheel like icon.

3. Hit that wheel like icon, and then tap/click **About Internet Explorer**

4. You will see an option **Install new version automatically**. Unmark the checkbox next to this option.

5. Tap/click **Close**

Now your IE 10 will not update on its own.

You can enable the auto update option whenever you want. Just follow the same steps and tick the checkbox next to **Install new version automatically.**

Make sure you are logged in as administrator before you make any such changes.

Tip # 43: Updating Windows Store

The Windows Store contains some of the most amazing apps. However to make the most of these apps, it is important that you update them regularly.

Developers of apps works for continuous improvement and whenever they fix the bugs or introduce any new features in their apps, they launch the updated version. You need to install the update in order to experience the advanced version of the particular app.

The best part here is that you don't need to manually update every app. All you need to do is enable the auto update feature and it will install the updates whenever there is one.

To activate the auto update tool,

1. Go the *Start Screen*

2. Tap/click the *Windows Store icon*

3. Now open the charms bar

4. Tap/click **Settings** > **App Updates**

5. If you are not yet logged in to the Windows Store, you will be asked to do at this point

6. Tap/click **Check for Updates**. Make sure you have turned on the **Automatically Download Updates For My Apps**.

7. Windows will check if there are any updates and will generate a list of all the apps that have new updates.

8. Tick the boxes next to the apps that you want to update

9. Tap/click **Install**

Tip # 44: Getting Familiar with the Windows Smart Screen

Windows SmartScreen is another very exciting feature of Windows 8. You surely don't want to miss it. Let us first tell you what it does and then we will move on to how you can enable it.

As mentioned several times before, Windows 8 is loaded with powerful data protection and security tools. Windows SmartScreen is an important component of this powerful security setup. The function of this tool is to alerts the user every time they attempt to download any potentially harmful or doubtful app from any unknown source.

To activate this remarkable safety feature,

1. Go to the *Control Panel > Action Center*

2. Tap/click **Windows SmartScreen settings**. You will find this option on the left side of the Action Center screen

3. Checkmark the circle next to **Get administrator approval before running an unrecognized application from the internet (recommended)**

4. Tap/click **OK**

You can deactivate the Windows SmartScreen later on however it is not recommended.

To deactivate the Windows SmartScreen,

1. Go to the *Control Panel > Action Center*

2. Tap/click **Windows SmartScreen settings**.

3. Checkmark the circle next to **Don't do anything (turn off Windows SmartScreen)**

4. Tap/click **OK**

Tip # 45: Activate the BitLocker

Just like Windows SmartScreen, BitLocker is another powerful security tool embedded in Windows 8. It allows you to protect your data by encrypting your fixed and removable drives.

It is not necessary to apply BitLocker on every drive. It is up to which drives you want to protect.

To enable BitLocker on any drive,

1. Right click the particular drive

2. Tap/click **Turn On BitLocker**

3. Tick the checkbox that says **Use a Password to Unlock the drive**

4. Enter your password (that can be easily remembered by you but not so easily guessed by others)

5. Create a backup recovery key and save it to your Microsoft account. You can also save it to any other external removable drive

6. Tap/click **Next**

7. Select how much of the particular drive you want to encrypt

8. Tap/click **Start encrypting**

9. It will take a couple of minutes for the encryption to complete.

10. Once it is done, restart your system.

Your drive is now encrypted and protected. You can encrypt other drives in the same manner.

Tip # 46: Getting Familiar with the SkyDrive

SkyDrive is a file transfer app. You can transfer any type of files to and from SkyDrive.

Here is how you can do this.

1. Go to *Start Screen*

2. Tap/click the *SkyDrive icon* (If you cannot find the SkyDrive live tile, just reveal the charm bar and type SkyDrive in the search bar)

3. Once the SkyDrive is opened, sign in to your Microsoft Account

4. Now right click anywhere on the SkyDrive screen

5. Tap/click **Upload**

6. Select the files that you want to transfer via SkyDrive

7. Tap/click **Add to SkyDrive**

The selected files will be transferred in a couple of seconds or minutes, depending upon the file size and the speed of your internet.

Tip # 47: Create a New User Account

Windows 8 allows you to create a number of user accounts. You can do so even after installing Windows 8.

There are two types of user accounts that you can create; Microsoft account and Local account.

As mentioned before, Microsoft account is the one that is based on the cloud server. You can access your account from any device having Windows 8. You just have to sign up for a Microsoft ID and password and that is all it is required to access your Microsoft account.

The other type of account, that is the Local account is device restricted. You can create and use it on only one device.

You can create a number of local as well Microsoft accounts. To create a new account in either category,

1. Go to Control Panel

2. Tap/click **Users**

3. Tap/click **Other Users** > **Add a User**

4. Select whether you want to create a *Local account* or *Microsoft account*

5. Follow the onscreen instructions to complete the account registration process.

You can create other accounts in the same way.

Tip # 48: How to Activate/Deactivate Windows Firewall

Windows 8 is very infamous for its numerous safety features. We have already discussed a few before; here is another one, the Windows Firewall. It protects your system from malware and virus attacks.

It is highly recommended that you enable the Windows Firewall and keep it enabled at all times, especially when you are online.

To activate Windows Firewall,

1. Log in as administrator, if you are logged in from any other account

2. Go to *Control Panel*

3. If you are using the large icons mode, Click/Tap **Windows Firewall**. If your control panel displays categories, Tap/Click **Systems and Security**

4. Tap/Click the checkbox next to **Turn on Windows Firewall.**

5. At times, the Windows also block some useful apps assuming them to be harmful. To see which apps are blocked, Tap/Click the checkbox next to **Notify me when Windows Firewall blocks a new app**

Follow the same procedure for turning off the Firewall.

Tip # 49: Restricting Kids Usage by Setting up Family Safety

Windows 8 contains some very high tech and useful features. The Family Safety feature is one of them. It allows you to restrict and monitor kid's usage on the computer. You can restrict your kids to access particular apps, websites and whatever is it that you don't want them to use.

To activate the Family Safety Feature in any user account,

1. Go to *Control Panel*

2. Tap/click **Family Safety**

3. You will see four categories; namely, Time Limits, *Windows Store and Game Restrictions, Web Filtering* and *App Restrictions*. Tap/Click on all of the mentioned categories to make the desired changes.

4. Save the changes

The changes will take effect immediately.

Now you can leave your kids unattended while they are using computer. They won't be able to access any app or site that you don't want them to. Just make sure your kids don't know the administrator account's password. Because the only way they can deactivate the Family Safety feature is by logging in as administrator.

Tip # 50: How to Copy and Move Files

The new and advanced File Explorer in Windows 8 allows you to copy and move your files very easily.

To move or copy a file from one window to another,

1. Click/Tap the particular item you want to copy. You can also select more than one item at a time.

2. Now Click/Tap the Home tab in your Windows Explorer

3. Tap/Click **Copy**. If you want to move the file(s), Tap/Click **Cut**

4. Go to the new destination of the selected file(s), where you want to move/copy them.

5. Tap/Click **Paste** from the Home tab of that new folder.

Tip # 51: Synchronize All Your Settings

One of the most popular and liked features of Windows 8 is that it keeps all your personal settings and preferences saved in the online Microsoft Servers. The best part is that you don't even have to save it, Windows 8 does so automatically.

The only requirement to activate and use this amazing feature of Windows 8 is to have a Microsoft Account, which many of us already have.

Remember, this facility is exclusive to Microsoft account holders only. All your settings, wallpapers, themes and files that are stored on your Microsoft account will automatically be synced and you can use them on any device having Windows 8. It does not apply to the local user accounts on your computer.

Tip # 52: Keep All Your Contacts in One Place

Windows 8 has made it real easy to keep all your contacts in one place. The built-in People app of Windows 8 is very comprehensive and user friendly.

To add a new contact,

1. Go the *Start Screen*

2. Click or tap the *People App*

3. Reveal the *Charms Bar*

4. Click/Tap **Settings**

5. Select **New contact**

6. Enter the name of your contact and other details

7. When you are done with it, Tap/click **Save**

Repeat the same process to add as many contacts you want. Just remember one thing: You will have to sign in to your Microsoft account to use the People app. All the contacts that you save in the device will be automatically saved in your Microsoft account. If you delete/remove the account from your computer, all the contacts saved in the People, Calendar and Mail apps will be deleted too.

Tip # 53: Create Backup and Stay Safe from Disk Crash

Have your computer ever gone through a disk crash? Well if it isn't, let us tell you what happens when a disk crashes. You lose all your files and data saved in that particular computer. Surely you don't want that to happen with you.

Well, don't worry. Windows 8 contains a backup feature that enables you to keep a backup of all your important data, in case the disk crashes.

Here is how you can use this amazing feature.

1. Go to **Control Panel**

2. Change the display to large icon mode

3. Click/Tap **Windows 7 File Recovery Option**

4. Select **Setup Backup Option**

5. Now wait for a few seconds till you see the *Windows Backup Utility*

6. Select a location for backup. t is recommended that you select any of your local drives and then move it to a removable drive later on.

7. After you select the backup drive, you will be prompted to choose the files you want to backup. You can either let Windows 8 select the files for you and you can do it manually. If you go for the latter option, a new window will open up asking you to select the files for backup.

8. Once you are done with it, Click/Tap **Settings**

9. Run the backup button

Once the backup process is completed, you can restore the selected files whenever you need.

Tip # 54: Find the Right Settings for Your System

You don't have to browse through all the settings to find the one you want to modify. Windows 8 allows you to search for the specific settings and go there directly.

Here is how you can do it.

1. Go to the *Start screen*

2. Reveal the *charms bar*

3. Type in the name of the setting you are looking for, such as display, privacy, keyboard or any other.

4. Windows 8 will search out the specific setting. Tap/click your desired search result.

You will be taken directly to that setting.

Tip # 55: Adjust the Size of Screen Tiles

This is another very interesting feature of Windows 8. You can very easily resize the tiles on the Start Screen. To do so,

1. Go to the *Start Screen*
2. Select the tile you want to resize
3. Right click to open the app commands
4. Tap/click **Larger** or **Smaller,** as per your preference. The size will be changed

Remember, you can resize every tile on Windows 8 Start Screen. However, most of them can be resized.

Tip # 56: Shortcut to Restart Windows 8

Many users find it hard to locate the power button in Windows 8. Well, you don't have to switch off your computer directly. All you have to do is hit the combination Alt + F4. As soon as you hit together these two keys, the shutdown/restart window will open up.

If you are not so good with shortcuts, here is also another way to restart Windows 8.

1. Go to the *Start Screen*

2. Click/Tap **Settings**

3. Click/Tap **Restart**

Tip # 57: Get To Know the Advanced IE 10

Internet Explorer has lost its fan base since the launch of Google Chrome. Though the former is still less popular than the atter, however the new IE 10 contains a number of great features that makes it the most secured web browser.

The most powerful feature of IE 10 is that the *'Do Not Track'* option is enabled by default. This implies that your personal data and browsing history is saved from tracking. No other websites would be able to track it unless to deactivate the *'Do Not Track'* option.

Apart from this, the Flip Ahead option of IE 10 has also gained immense popularity. With this option enabled, you can browse the web as if you are reading a book. The best part is that IE 10 automatically searches for the forward buttons on the webpage. You don't need to click/tap any link cr tab to go to the next page.

There are two versions of IE 10.

1. Metro Version

2. Desktop Version

You can switch between the two as per your preference.

Tip # 58: Personalize the Taskbar

You can easily rearrange the icons on the taskbar. All you have to do is select drag the particular icon or button from its current position and drop it to the new location.

And this is not just it! Windows 8 even allow you to change the position of your taskbar. Here is how you can do this.

1. First you need to unlock your taskbar. You can do this by removing the small tick mark next to it.

2. After you remove the tick mark, click/tap and hold any empty space in the task bar and drag it to any of the four corners on the screen.

3. Once the taskbar reaches its new location, you can release your hold.

Tip # 59: Windows 8 Task Manager

Windows Task Manager is the most helpful feature in all the versions of Windows. Almost every Windows user is familiar with it. It is mostly used to close the applications or processes that are not responding.

The Windows Task Manager of Windows 8 is better than all its predecessors. It is very simple and user friendly. It does not show any long list of apps and complicated technical details. No extra menus or unnecessary tabs. It shows only the basic information needed by a standard Windows user.

If any of your app is not working properly or you see a *Not Responding* error appears at the top of the page, all you have to do is open the *Task Manager* and click/tap the **End Task** button in front of the particular app or program.

Here is how you can open the Task Manager in Windows 8,

1. Reveal the charms bar

2. Type **Task Manager** in the search box

3. Tap/click **Task Manager** in the search results

If you are using a mouse, then take the cursor to the lower left corner of your screen. Right-click to open the advanced commands and then select *Task Manager*.

Just remember one thing before you kill any application or process in the Task Manager. That is the Task Manager does not warn you to save your work before it kills the application. So it is your responsibility to first save your work and then kill the particular app or process.

Tip # 60: How to Connect To Wi-Fi in Windows 8

Windows 8 has a very powerful Wi-Fi detector. You just need to activate it.

To connect Wi-Fi in Windows 8,

1. Reveal the *Charms Bar*

2. Tap/Click **Settings**

3. Select the *Wireless icon*

4. Windows 8 will scan and generate the list of available Wi-Fi networks

5. Select your *Wi-Fi network*

6. Tap/Click **Connect**

7. Enter your Wi-Fi password and Click/Tap **Next**

8. Windows 8 will verify the password and if it is correct, it will establish the Internet connect to the particular Wi-Fi network.

Tip # 61: Pin Your Favorite Apps

Windows 8 allows you to pin your favorite apps to the Start Screen for quick and easy access. It is just like making a shortcut of on the desktop.

Here is how you can do it.

1. Locate the app or folder on your system that you want to pin to that Start Screen

2. Right-click the particular app to open the advanced app commands.

3. Tap/Click **Pin to Start**

The particular app will be pinned to your Start Screen. Likewise, you can pin other apps also.

Tip # 62: The 'Multiple Windows' Feature

Now this is a very interesting feature of Windows 8. It allows you to work with multiple apps and on more than one window at the same time.

If you want to use this incredible feature of Windows 8, hit and hold **Alt + Tab** if you are using a keyboard. If you are using mouse, then take the cursor to the top left corner of your screen and click it.

Once you do it, all the opened apps and pages on your system will cascade on your screen. You can view and work on them at the same time on the same screen.

Now isn't amazing?

Tip # 63: Getting Familiar with the Charms Bar

The Charm Bar is perhaps the most famous and liked feature of Windows 8. It is one the things that make Windows 8 stand apart its predecessors. It contains shortcuts to several commonly used features.

The *Search* tab in the charms bar enables you to search for any file or app on your system. Just type in the name and it will find it for you.

Then there is this *Share* tab. It allows you to share your photos, videos and Facebook statuses with friends. The Share feature of the charm bar is very popular especially among youngsters who like to share every moment of their life on Facebook.

The *Start* tab of the charm bar performs two functions:

1. If you are on any other screen, tap/click **Start** to directly go back to the start screen.

2. If you are already on the start screen, tap/click **Start** to go back to the last app or page you were using.

The *Device* charm allows you to manage all the devices connected to your system. And then finally there is the Settings charm. It provides you quick access to your computer's setting.

Well, this was just a brief overview of the infamous Windows 8 charms. To explore more, reveal the charms bar by swiping from the right edge of your to the left side.

If you are using Windows 8 on computer or laptop, then take the cursor to the right side of your screen and move it up or down to open up the incredible charms bar.

Tip # 64: How to Print PDF Documents

Printing PDF files with Windows 8 is very easy. Here is how you can do this.

1. Open the PDF file that you want to print

2. Hit Ctrl + P

3. Click/tap the printer icon to modify the print settings

4. Tap/click Print to send the print command

Tip # 65: Windows 8 'Optimize Drives Tool'

Just like the shutdown button, many people find it hard to locate the Disk Defragmenter in Windows 8.

Well, here is the secret. The Disk Defragmenter is still there, but with the name of Optimize Drives tool.

Just reveal the *Select* charms and type *Optimize Drives*. Even if you type in Disk Defragmenter, it will still locate the Optimize Drives tool for you.

Tip # 66: Zoom In and Zoom Out

Now this is another very interesting feature of Windows 8. It allows you to increase or decrease the size of the webpage.

To zoom in and zoom out of the webpage, all you have to do is click the small arrow next to the Change Zoom Level button (resembles a magnifying glass).

You can also do this with a keyboard.

1. To zoom in, hit Ctrl + plus key

2. To zoom out, hit Ctrl + minus key

The above procedure applies to computers and laptops containing Windows 8. If you are using a touch-screen device, you have to use your two fingers to zoom in or zoom out.

1. To magnify the screen or webpage, place two fingers on the screen close to each other and then pinch outwards.

2. To decrease the size of the screen, place two fingers on the screen slightly apart each other and then squeeze inwards.

Tip # 67: Enjoy Watching Your Favorite Videos in Windows 8

Windows 8 is a multi-purpose OS. Not only is it good for work purpose, but it is an amazing entertainment tool as well.

The Video app in Windows 8 is a full-on fun tool. You can enjoy your favorite videos, TV shows and stream movies from the amazing Xbox Video app.

To open the Windows 8 Video app,

1. Reveal the Charms bar

2. Select **Search**

3. Type **Video**

4. Tap/click **Video** in the search results

5. Tap/click your favorite movie or video to watch it.

Tip # 68: Tips for Increased Protection

Windows 8 features the powerful IE 10 which is fully loaded with security and protection tools. Now you can browse, share, email, buy and perform all the online activities absolutely carefree.

Here are a few tips to ensure the optimum usage of IE 10 security features.

1. It is highly recommended that you open InPrivate browsing in IE 10, especially when you are opening a website that requires you to enter your password. The InPrivate browsing feature will restrict Internet Explorer to save the password or search history.

2. If you are not very comfortable with the InPrivate browsing, then make sure to delete manually all the browsing history when you exit. All you have to do is go to **Internet Options > Delete your browsing history**. It will clear all your cache, temporary files, saved forms, saved passwords, cookies and other browsing details.

3. Even if you don't take any precautions while browsing, IE 10 does it for you. The *SmartScreen Filter* and the *Do Not Track feature* is activated by default in Internet Explorer 10. These two tools provide you added protection as soon as you open the IE 10 browser.

Tip # 69: Stay Updated With the Stock Market

Students, teachers, bankers, investors or any other profession, Windows 8 has something to offer for every field of business. The Finance app contains the recent finance-related news and up-to-date status of the market.

The built-in Finance app that we are talking about can be found on the Windows 8 Metro interface. It even has a Live Tile that shows the updated statistics of Dow Jones, NASDAQ and S&P.

If you want to keep track of some particular stocks, you can feed their names in the Finance app and it will keep you updated with the specified stocks and their underlying market.

The most amazing part is that this app is free of any charge. You can stay in touch with all the market happenings without having to pay a cent.

Tip # 70: Accessing Technical Details of the Apps

As we have already explained in Tip # 59, Windows 8 Task Manager is very simple. It does not show any complicated technical details that mostly confuses an average user. But it does not mean that Windows 8 is not for tech savvies and those who understand all the technical details.

The Task Manager is very simple on the face. However, if you want to see any technical details, tap/click **Details** and it will show you all the information about the processes and apps that are currently running your system.

Tip # 71: Enable Add-Ons

If you want to use the add-ons of IE 10 in Windows 8, you will have to switch to the Desktop version (refer to Tip # 19 to learn how to switch to the Desktop view).

Once you are on the Desktop version, simply click the small gear-resembling settings button located in the top right edge of your screen. Doing so will enable the add-ons in Internet Explorer 10.

Tip # 72: Modify the Default Programs

Windows 8 allows you to choose a default program for certain apps and files. In other words, you can command your Windows 8 to always open the specific apps such as music, video and image files in a particular format.

Suppose you want to see all your images in JPEG format, now you can set this as the default program for the Image app. Once you do this, all the images will be directly opened in JPEG format unless directed otherwise.

To set your default program,

1. Reveal the *Charms Bar*

2. Select **Search**

3. Enter Default Programs in the search bar

4. Click/tap **Default Programs**

5. Click/tap **Set your default programs**

6. Now select the program you want to set as Default

7. Click/tap **Set this program as default**

You can also customize these settings further if you want. For example, if you want a program to open any particular file type, then Click/tap **Choose defaults for this program.**

You can change these settings later on whenever you want.

Tip # 73: Different Versions of Windows 8

At present, there are four different versions of Windows 8.

1. Windows 8

2. Windows 8 Pro

3. Windows 8 Enterprise

4. Windows 8 RT

As the name suggest, Windows 8 Enterprise is especially meant for business enterprises.

Windows 8 RT is for tablets and other such devices.

Windows 8 Pro is for professionals and tech savvies.

The most common and preferred among all is the simple Windows 8. It is perfect for standard users, those who are not too tech savvy and not familiar with the technicalities of the operating system.

Tip # 74: Not Responding? Kill the App

You are working on a very important file or watching your favorite movie and suddenly it hangs and displays a note at the top left saying *Not Responding*. This is the most annoying situation for every Windows user.

Frozen and unresponsive programs are very irritating and the worst part is that you cannot get rid of them completely. You can try to lower their frequency of occurring by incorporating some security and performance boosting measures, however no app or software can guarantee that that you won't ever encounter any unresponsive program.

Well don't worry! The simplest way to deal with a frozen program is to kill it. Just hit and hold **Ctrl + Alt + Del** at the same time. Doing so will open the Task Manager. Choose the unresponsive program and then click **End Task** to close it instantly.

If still nothing happens and the underlying app is frozen, hit and hold the power button till your system shuts down. Wait for a couple of minutes the turn it on. This should get rid of the unresponsive app.

Tip # 75: Do Not Miss Your Appointments

To add an appointment or any other important meeting to your Calder app,

1. Open the *Calendar App*

2. Right-click anywhere on the Calendar. This will open up the App bar

3. Click/tap **New**

4. Set the reminder for your meeting/appointment.

5. Enter your active email address, feed the other required details and hit **Save**

Your appointment will now appear in your email account.

If you want to edit any of your calendar appointments,

1. Open the *Calendar App*

2. Right-click anywhere on the Calendar. This will open up the App bar

3. Select the Edit icon

4. Make the desired modifications and click **Save**.

Tip # 76: Choose Your Own Power Plan

The advanced *Windows 8 power plans* gives you the power to control the way your PC or tablet consumes power.

There are different power plans depending upon the specs of your computer or laptop. Here is how you can find out which power plans are available for your device.

1. Go to *Control Panel*

2. Tap/click **Power Options**

3. You can choose from the options that are made available by your PC manufacturer. Normally the power plans include Power Saver, Balanced or High Performance.

You can also select a power plan by clicking the small battery icon in the notification panel.

If you don't find a power plan of your preference, make one for your own. Windows 8 allows you to create your own power plan. To do this,

1. Go to *Control Panel*

2. Tap/click **Power Options**

3. Tap/click **Create a Power Plan**

4. Modify the power settings and save the changes

Tip # 77: Select Multiple Files

You can copy, move, delete or perform any other function simultaneously to more than one file.

To select multiple files in the Windows Explorer, simply hit and hold the Ctrl key. Now select as many files as you want, just make sure you are holding down the Ctrl key while you are selecting files.

Once you are done clicking all files, let go of the Ctrl key and perform the desired command on the selected files.

Tip # 78: Personalize the Icons

Now you can change the icons for folders in Windows 8. It is pretty easy and interesting too. Here is how you can do this.

1. First you need to right click on the desired folder

2. A small menu will appear on your screen. Select **Properties** from this menu.

3. Hit the **Customize** tab

4. Tap/click **Change Icon**.

5. Now this is the interesting part. As soon as you hit the change icon button, a new window will open up on your screen containing all the icons that you can use.

6. Choose the desired icon and then hit **OK**

The particular folder will now be represented with the selected icon.

Tip # 79: Dance to Your Favorite Tunes

To listen to your favorite songs, Go to the *Start Screen* > Tap/click the *Music app.* It will generate the list of songs saved in your computer. Hit the one you want to listen.

Here is another way to open the music app if you cannot find it on your Start Screen.

1. Reveal the charms bar.

2. Select *Search* and enter *Music* in the search bar.

3. Select music from the search results.

4. Tap/click the song you want to listen and enjoy.

You can also browse and listen to the new songs and other classic hits by using the Xbox music feature in the Music app. Open up the Xbox, search for the desired song or album and hit play.

If you want enjoy ad-free music streaming, all you have to do it get yourself an Xbox Music Pass and you will be able to listen your favorite songs without being interrupted by any annoying ads.

Tip # 80: Activate the Windows Defender

The Windows Defender is another powerful member of the Windows 8 fully loaded security system. It shields your system from hazardous virus attacks, malicious malware and other potentially harmful software. However to use this amazing security tool, it is imperative that you keep it turned on at all times.

To use the Windows Defender in Windows 8,

1. Reveal the *Charms Bar*

2. Select **Search**

3. Type *Windows Defender* in the search bar

4. Tap/click **Windows Defender** in the search results

5. Once it is opened, Hit **Settings**

6. Mark the checkbox next to **Turn on real-time protection (recommended)**

7. Tap/click **Save Changes**

It is highly recommended that you run the Windows Defender Scan on regular basis. To do so, simply open up the *Windows Defender*. Select the *home tab* and hit **Scan now.** It will detect and delete all the virus and malware in your system, if there are any.

Tip # 81: Windows 8 and the Remote Desktop App

Windows 8 features the advanced Remote Desktop app that allows you to connect your system to a remote PC from almost anywhere.

To use the incredible Remote Desktop app,

1. Go to the *Metro Version (Live Tiles Screen)*

2. Locate the Remote Desktop app and tap/click to open it.

3. Enter the name of the PC to which you want to connect. Make sure you enter the exact name of the remote PC. If you don't know it, open **Computer** > **Properties**. There you will find the name of the computer. Jot it down.

4. After you enter the computer's name in the Remote Desktop app, you will be asked to enter the email ID and password of the same computer.

5. Tap/Click **Connect**

6. It will take a few minutes for the connection to establish successfully. After it is done, you will see the login ID and other details of the remote PC.

Tip # 82: Interactive Mouse Gestures

Here are a few interesting and useful mouse shortcuts for Windows 8.

1. To see your customized settings for the current app, right-click at the top of your Start Screen

2. To enable semantic zoom, simply hit and hold the Ctrl key while you scroll up or down the mouse.

3. To see the list of all the currently opened apps, just point your cursor to the top left corner of the screen and then move it down.

Tip # 83: Pin to Taskbar

In Tip # 61, we revealed a way of pinning apps to the Start Screen. Well, you can also do the same to taskbar.

Pinning your frequently used apps to the taskbar will save you from the hassle of searching them every time you want to use them.

To pin your favorite apps to the taskbar,

1. Locate the particular app

2. Right-click the app

3. Tap/click **Pin this program to taskbar**

4. The specified app will now appear in the taskbar.

Tip # 84: Personalize Your Screen's Appearance

You can personalize the appearance of your Lock Screen as well your Start Screen in Windows 8.

Here is how you can do it.

1. Go to *PC settings* (Settings Charm)

2. Click/tap **Personalize**

3. Select **Start Screen**

4. Make the desired changes. You can select a preset pattern, theme and color.

5. Now Select **Lock Screen**

6. Make the desired changes

7. Hit **Save** for the changes to take effect.

Tip # 85: Explore the Photos App

Windows 8 contains innumerous fun features, one of which is its built-in photo app. It not only allows you to view and share your photos and videos, but you can also view pictures and videos from several other popular social networking forums including Flickr, Facebook and SkyDrive.

You can find the Photo app on the Metro Start Screen.

You can also import any graphics or such files from your camera or any other removable drive. If you want to do this,

1. First you need to connect the particular device to your computer/tablet.

2. Now open the Photos app and swipe down from the top of your screen (you can also swipe up from the bottom of the screen).

3. Tap/click **Import**. All the selected photos and videos will be transferred to the Photo App.

Tip # 86: Find Your Missing Apps

Don't worry if you are unable to find any of your important apps, files or folders, or it se are missing. Just reveal the Charms bar, select Search and type in the name of the file or folder you are looking for. The Windows 8 will check every bit of your system for the particular file.

If the search charm is unable to locate your file, check the File History. You are surely going to find it there. Refer to Tip # 88 to learn more about File History.

Tip # 87: Delete and Restore

The bad thing is that Windows 8 does not warn you when you delete any file. If you want to delete any file or folder, just select the particular file and hit **Delete** on the File Explorer menu.

Now the good thing is that these files are not permanently deleted. The files that you delete are sent to the recycle bin. You can go the recycle bin and restore the particular files in case you have deleted them accidently.

Tip # 88: Turning on the File History Feature

File History comes to your rescue in case you are unable to find any file and the Search charm is also not able to hunt it down. But first you need to turn on the File History tool.

Here is how you can do this.

1. Reveal the *charms bar*

2. Select **Search**

3. Enter File History in the search bar

4. Tap/click **File History** in the search results

5. Tap/click **Turn on**

6. To restore your lost files, head to *PC settings*

7. Tap/click **Restore your files with File History**

8. Enter the name of the particular file in the search bar. If you don't remember the name, you can also explore the folders.

9. Once you find your file, select it

10. Tap/click **Restore**

Tip # 89: Access the Control Panel

Control panel is the gateway to almost all the features and advanced settings. And just like the power button, the traditional tab of control panel is missing in Windows 8. Nevertheless you can always find it via the Search charm.

Just reveal the *Charms Bar*, select **Search**, enter *Control Panel* and select **Control Panel** from the search results.

Tip # 90: Reveal the Ribbons

To open the ribbon in Windows 8, all you have to do it open 'Computer' or *'My Computer'* and hit the tiny arrow beside the question mark. This will reveal the ribbon instantly.

Tip # 91: Splitting the Screen in Windows 8

You can split the screens on tablets and other touch-screen devices containing Windows 8.

This can be done when two or more windows or apps are opened or running in the background. You can split the screens and view all of them at the same time. You can even split the metro and desktop screens.

To activate the amazing split screen feature,

1. First touch the app or window at the left side of the screen

2. Now hold it and drag it to the right side of the screen

After you do this, you will see a split screen with the desktop version on one side and Metro app on the other side.

Tip # 92: Post Installation Unlocking

After the successful installation of Windows 8 in your computer or tablet, you will come across the Lock Screen. You will have to pass this screen to access your system. Here is how you can do this.

1. If you are using a keyboard, all you have to do it hit the space bar to unlock the Lock Screen.

2. If you are using mouse, simply spin your mouse wheel to pass through the Lock Screen.

3. If you are using a touch-screen device, swipe upwards from the bottom to unlock the Lock Screen.

Now enter the username and password that you created during the installation process and you will be taken to the Start screen.

Tip # 93: Improving the Screen Resolution

If you are encountering frozen or unresponsive apps too frequently, try changing the resolution of your screen.

To improve the screen resolution,

1. Right-click anywhere on your desktop

2. Click/tap **Screen Resolution**

3. Increase the settings slightly to improve the screen resolution.

Perhaps this will sort out the frozen apps problem.

Tip # 94: Two Windows – One System

If you are still skeptical about Windows 8 and want to try it first before getting rid of your old Windows, it is absolutely possible.

Following is the step by step process on how you can use the two versions of Windows on one computer or laptop. For the sake of understanding, here we have assumed the old version to be Windows 7.

1. First, you need to create a partition where you can install Windows 8

2. In Windows 7, hit the *Windows key*

3. Type **partitions**

4. Select **Create and format hard drive partitions**

5. Now you will have to cut down on Drive C and then create the new partition.

6. Once you are done with the partition, insert the Windows 8 installation DVD/USB.

7. When you start the installation process, make sure to select the new partition for installation.

8. Once Windows 8 are successfully installed in the new partition, restart your system.

Now you will be given an option to use Windows 8 or Windows 7. These options will appear every time you boot your system.

Tip # 95: Windows 8 and Windows Snap

If you want to explore the full screen features of Metro applications, you must try Snap. It allows you to snap an app into the thin sidebar at the same time allowing another app to take place on the screen.

Snap is only possible with Metro apps since they are written in HTML5 and CSS and can therefore adapt to the thin sidebar space. Just make sure the screen resolution is at least 1,366 x 768 pixels in order to use the Snap feature.

Also you need Regedit if you want to snap any app. Find it through the search charm. Once you are there, open the folder named as follows:

HKEY_CURRENT_USER\Software\Microsoft\Windows\CurrentVersion\ImmersiveShell\AppPositioner

If the particular folder is not there, simply create it.

Once you get to this folder, you will find a switch named **AlwaysEnableLSSnapping**. Set it to 1.

And you are ready to snap now!

Tip # 96: Get Familiar with the People Application

The People app of Windows 8 integrates the phone address book and the social networking accounts. This app is mainly divided into three parts namely; the People View, the What's New Section and the Me Page.

The *People View* contains the list of all your contacts that you manually fed into the address book as well all those that you synced via email, Facebook and other social networking accounts.

Then there is this *What's New* section. It is the combined newsfeed of all your social networking accounts. You can tweet, re-tweet, post status on Facebook and manage all your social networking accounts through one place.

Finally there is this *Me Page*. It contains the highlights of your activities on your social networking accounts.

Tip # 97: Are Certain Notifications Distracting You?

There are several apps that post notifications every time there is an update. If you find these notifications distracting, you can turn them off.

There are two ways of restricting the notifications:

1. Go to the Settings Charm and disable notifications for as long as you want.

2. Go to the Settings Charm. Select Pc Settings > Notifications. There you can disable the notifications of the desired apps.

The second way is better if you want to receive notifications from certain specified apps.

Tip # 98: Using Virtual Machines

Have you ever used Virtual Machines? Well, these are simulated computers that run as an app on your desktop.

Windows 8 allows you to use Virtua machines. If you have installed the Windows 8 ISO file, command your virtual machine manager to use it as the system's optical drive. Now follow the installation procedure and on-screen instructions to use Virtual machines without making any modifications to your system.

Tip # 99: Group Your Apps

Is your Start Screen a mess, loaded with apps, folders and pinned files? Well then, why not take advantage of the integrated grouping tools to categories all the files and place them into respective folders. The built-in organization tool helps you divide all the icons on the Start Screen into neatly labeled groups.

Here is how you can do this.

1. Select all the tiles and icons that you want to place in one folder.

2. Now drag all of the selected tiles to the right hand edge of your screen. Make sure the spot where you drag these files is vacant.

3. The built-in organization tool will sequester the particular tiles together

4. Once you are satisfied with the grouping, use semantic zoom peek your desktop

5. Now select the newly formed group and right click on it.

6. Select **Name group**

7. Give name to the particular group.

There you go. Enjoy your neatly organized Start Screen.

Tip # 100: Save Network Bandwidth with Windows 8

Live Tiles are very useful and accommodating. However there is only con to it and that is they use lots of network bandwidth. Even this should be not be an issue unless you have a limited bandwidth or are using metered connection.

Well, it doesn't mean that users running on metered connection should not use Live Tiles. Windows 8 has a solution for this dilemma too.

Here is what you need to do to save your network bandwidth.

1. Go to the Taskbar

2. Select your network connection

3. Right-click your network conrection

4. Select **Set as metered connection**

Windows 8 will now restrict the usage of individual Live Tiles. Also it will only download the priority Windows updates.

If you want to want these settings, right-click your connection again and select **Set as unmetered**.